OUR AMAZING WORLD

# BEARS

Kay de Silva

*Aurora*

# Contents

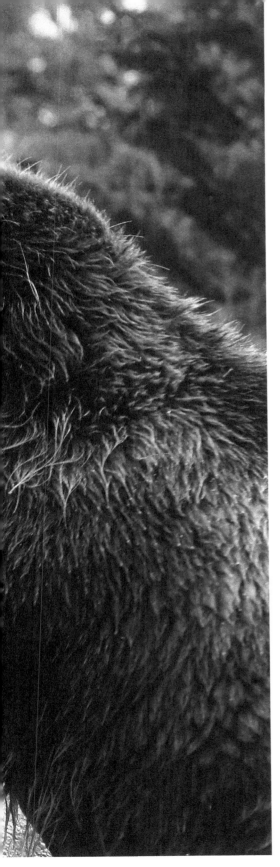

# DEFENCE

Although bears are peace-loving, bear *confrontations* or fights can be very brutal. A confrontation will often end up in death or serious injury. Bears, however, act defensively before they attack.

A *defensive* bear will behave in a certain way. It may growl, huff, or swing its head from side to side. It may rise to its full height on its hind legs and fluff its fur or turn sideways. This is to make it look bigger in the eyes of its enemies.

It may also walk around with stiffened front legs or slap one or two feet around or on the ground. In addition, it may also quickly open and close its mouth. This is known as *jaw popping*.

*Squabbles over food often come to gruesome endings.*

*A Bear sleeping peacefully in its den.*

# HIBERNATION

During the cold winter months some animals become inactive and fall into a deep, sleep-like state. This is known as *hibernation*. Hibernation helps animals save energy during winter when food is not easily available. During these times animals slowly use stored body fat to survive.

It is said that bears are not true *hibernators*. This is because unlike true hibernators, a bear's temperature drops slightly and the bear is easily awakened, so this bear activity is called *winter sleep*.

Not all bears fall into a winter sleep. This depends on where they live. Bears that live in habitats where it is warm and who have plenty of food all year round do not need winter sleep.

*A Bear couple meandering through a meadow.*

# MATING

Male bears are called *boars*, and females are called *sows*. Bears that live in warmer climates mate all year round. Others mate during spring.

When mating is complete, boars go away. Most boars never see the sow again. Neither do they see their cubs.

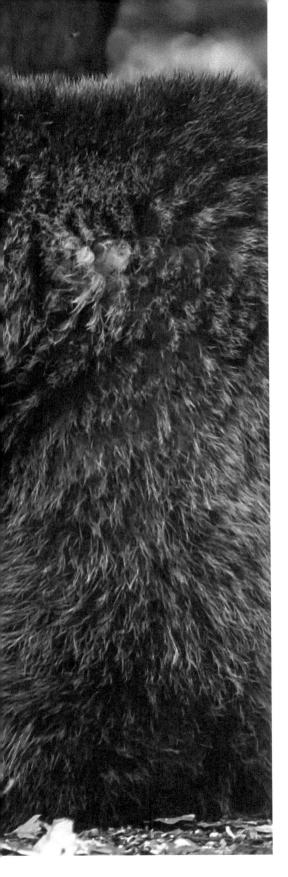

# BEAR CUBS

After 3 to 6 months inside their mother, baby bears are born. Baby bears are called *cubs*. They are born tiny and helpless. A newborn is about the size of a kitten.

At first these toothless cubs are unable to see or hear. Bear cubs depend on their mother to feed and protect them. In the first few months, cubs feed only on their mother's milk. In the early days bear cubs are usually carried by the scruff of their necks.

When cubs are older, they must follow their mother and learn to find food and hunt. Cubs stay with their mother for about 2 years. She then sends them away to live on their own. Sometimes siblings continue to stay together for another year or so to protect each other.

*Apple of her eye: A mother bear will protect her cub with her life.*

*An American Black Bear in the Snowy Mountains, USA, enjoying a snack.*

# AMERICAN BLACK BEARS

*American Black Bears* are the most commonly found bears in the world. They live in the mountain forests of North America.

Despite their name, these bears come in a variety of colors. Some American black bears have black fur, while others have brown or silvery-blue fur. The *Kermode Bear*, a type of American Black Bear is known to produce pure white-furred bears.

American Black Bears are *opportunistic omnivores*. This means that they will eat anything that they find. Their diets change every season. They love carrion. When they cannot find meat, they eat insects, grasses, roots, berries, and nuts.

*A howling Asiatic Black Bear.*

# ASIATIC BLACK BEARS

*Asiatic Black Bears* are also known as the *Moon Bears of Tibet*. This is because of the white crescent-shaped mark found on their chests. These bears can be found in the forests of Northern Pakistan, Iran, Afghanistan, and the mountain regions of Eastern Asia.

Asiatic Black Bears are omnivores. They eat carrion, insects, fruit, berries, and honey. They sometimes peel the bark of trees to eat the exposed wood sap. They also enjoy eating nuts.

They use forked branches on trees to build platforms. These platforms are called bear's nests. Made of twigs and leaves, they look like birds' nests. Here bears sit and feed comfortably.

# GIANT PANDA BEARS

*Giant Panda Bears* are probably the most unusual of all bears. They are found only in 6 areas of China. These bears were previously thought of as a species of raccoon. They are now considered bears. Despite their names, Giant Panda Bears are small bears.

Bamboo shoots and leaves are Pandas' main food. They may, however, occasionally eat other types of vegetation, fish, and animals. Bamboo is not a nutritious meal, so to be healthy Pandas eat fast and a lot. Adult Pandas spend up to 12 hours eating about 50 pounds (22 kilograms) of bamboo every day.

*A Giant Panda Bear chowing down.*

# GRIZZLY BEARS

Grizzly Bears are *Brown Bears* that are found in North America. Their thick fur can vary from light brown to almost black. They get their name from the silver-tipped hairs they get as they grow older. These hairs give them a grizzling or greying appearance.

Grizzly Bears are much larger than Black Bears. Male Grizzlies stand about 7 feet (2 meters) tall and weigh between 300 and 600 pounds (135 and 270 kilograms). Despite their size they can run up to a speed of 30 mph (miles per hour).

Grizzlies' winter sleep lasts about 5 to 8 months. They prepare for it by gaining up to 400 pounds (180 kilograms) during warmer months. They also dig themselves a den, usually on a mountainside to keep safe from predators.

*A Grizzly Bear taking a snooze.*

*A close encounter with a magnificent Kodiak Bear.*

# KODIAK BEARS

*Kodiak Bears* are *Brown Bears* that are found only on the *Kodiak Archipelago*. It is believed that these bears migrated there from Alaska over 12,000 years ago.

Kodiak Bears are the largest bears in the world. Male bears stand over 10 feet (3 meters) tall and weigh as much as 1,500 pounds (680 kilograms). This is heavier than 10 people weighed together.

Kodiak Bears are known as the largest land *carnivores*. Their favorite food is salmon. In the spring, however, they are known to eat nuts, fruits, and berries. So Kodiak Bears, like many other bears, are really omnivores.

*Also known as the "Honey Bear," the Malayan Sun Bear uses its long tongue to extract honey.*

# MALAYAN SUN BEARS

*Malayan Sun Bears* are found in the tropical rainforests of Southeast Asia. These bears wear a loose coat of sleek black fur. They get their name from the U-shaped patch of orange fur found on their chests. According to Malayan folktales, this marking is a mark of the rising sun.

Despite their name, Sun Bears are nocturnal. This means that they are active at night and sleep in the day. They lumber through the forests at night eating fruits, roots, insects, small lizards, and rodents. They use their long claws that are over 4 inches (10 centimeters) to rip open trees and slurp up termites with their extra-long tongues.

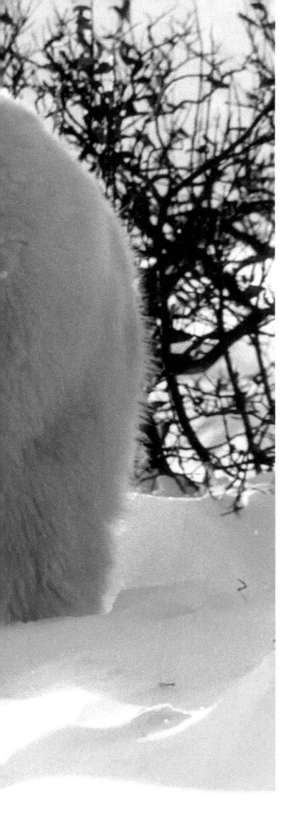

# POLAR BEARS

*Polar Bears* live in the icy lands and freezing waters of the Arctic Circle. They have unique bodies that suit this environment. Blubber, a thick layer of fat, protects their bodies from the cold.

These bears are known as the most carnivorous of all bears. Great hunters, they enjoy seals, walruses, and beached whales.

*A Polar Bear and her cubs in low Arctic sunlight.*

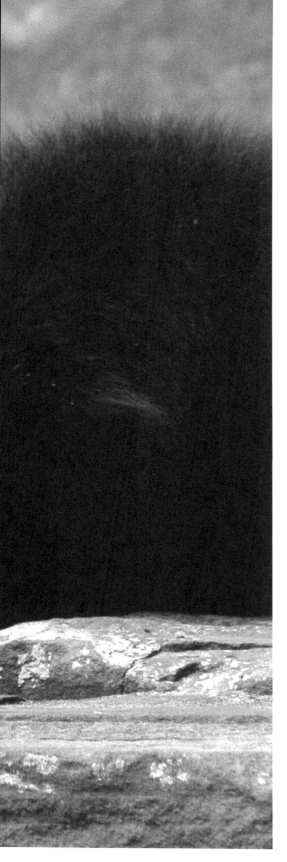

# SLOTH BEARS

*Sloth Bears* are found in Southeast Asia. They mostly live in the forest areas of India and Sri Lanka. Sloth Bears used to be confused with *Sloths*. This is because both animals behave in a similar way. Like Sloths, Sloth Bears like to hang on tree branches. Unlike Sloths, however, Sloth Bears are fast and agile.

Like Sloths, Sloth Bear mamas give their cubs piggyback rides. Unlike other bear species, these boars stay to look after their cubs. Because they are nocturnal, they sleep by day and travel and feed by night.

These bears feed mostly on termites. They have no front teeth but have long snouts, flexible and hairless lips, and closing nostrils, which makes them perfect termite hunters. They can be heard around 300 feet (90 meters) away sucking up termites from their mounds. What they miss when slurping, they scoop up with their long tongues.

*A Sloth Bear nursing her cubs.*

# SPECTACLED BEARS

*Spectacled Bears* live in the Andes Mountains. They are also known as *Andean Bears*. The circular white or yellow markings around their eyes give these bears their name.

Spectacled Bears eat fruits, grasses, berries, and honey. Sometimes they eat meat, such as small rodents, birds, and insects. Like Asiatic Black Bears, they, too, build bear nests. They are known to sit in their nests waiting for fruit to ripen.

*A Spectacled Bear in the wilderness.*

*One of only a thousand existing Pandas sleeping contentedly in a conservation center.*

# BEAR NECESSITY

Like all animals, bears play an important role in the eco-system. As hunters, bears cull weak and sick animals. As scavengers, they eat carrion, so they clean up the environment and stop diseases from spreading. They also roam across large territories, scattering undigested plant seeds. In this way they help bring new life.

Bears are often thought of as scary animals. Bears, however, become aggressive only when they feel threatened. Sadly, human activity such as hunting, deforestation, and global warming threatens the habitats and existence of these magnificent creatures.

# OUR AMAZING WORLD
## COLLECT THEM ALL

WWW.OURAMAZINGWORLDBOOKS.COM

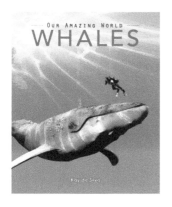
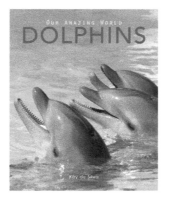
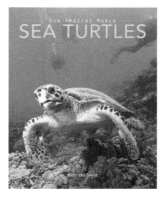
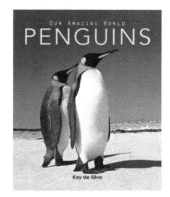

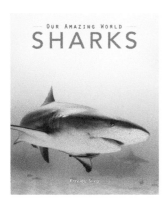
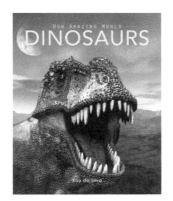
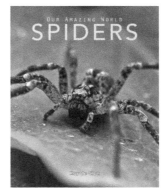
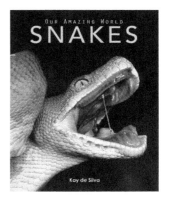

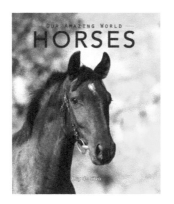

Aurora
An imprint of CKTY Publishing Solutions

ouramazingworldbooks.com

Text copyright © Kay de Silva, 2013
The moral right of the author has been asserted

ISBN 978-0-9946009-3-6

1, volkova natalia/Shutterstock; 2-3, Erik Mandre/Shutterstock; 5, Neelsky/Shutterstock; 8, Scott E Read/
Shutterstock; 9, IamCDN/BigStock; 10-11, Zixian/BigStock; 12-13, PhotoBarmaley/Shutterstock; 14-15,
Coffee999/BigStock; 16, Elwynn/BigStock; 17, FlorianA/BigStock; 18-19, Un.bolovan/Shutterstock; 20,
L.A.Waterhouse/BigStock; 21, Ostill/BigStock; 22-23, LeungChopan/BigStock; 24-25, Zoran/BigStock; 26,
Dzain/BigStock; 27, 30-31, Wrangel/BigStock; 28-29, Outdoorsman/Shutterstock;
32-33, Lighttraveler/Shutterstock; 34, SJ Travel Photo and Video/Shutterstock

Printed in the USA
CPSIA information can be obtained
at www.ICGtesting.com
LVHW071405070923
757520LV00020B/693